LOUVRE

# LOUVRE

Pierre Quoniam

**Inspecteur général
honoraire des musées de France**

**Ministère de la Culture, de la Communication,
des Grands Travaux et du Bicentenaire**

**Editions de la Réunion des musées nationaux**

# Contents

6

**Preface**

8

**The Louvre Palace and Museum**

14

**Oriental Antiquities**

22

**Egyptian Antiquities**

Design : *Grapus 89 .* Pierre Bernard, Fokke Draaijer

Translation : B. Shuey and A. Roberts

ISBN : 2-7118-2231-1 (French edition)
ISBN : 2-7118-2232-X (English edition)

32

**Greek, Etruscan and Roman Antiquities**

46

**Paintings**

88

**Graphic Arts**

90

**Sculptures**

102

**Decorative Arts**

# Preface

*In memory of Pierre Quoniam*

The collections in the seven departments of the Louvre museum, each one of which corresponds to a chapter in this book, together make up a composite history of human artistic creation.

The three departements of antiquities show how the great civilisations of The Middle East, Egypt and the Mediterranean emerged and blossomed, from the third millennium before the birth of Christ until the first centuries of the Christian era. After this, the museum's four 'modern' departments trace the development of European art from the high middle ages to the 19th century, with separate emphasis on the evolution of sculpture, the decorative arts, painting and graphic arts.

Is the Louvre's version of the history of art complete, and if so, is it entirely impartial? The answer to both questions is emphatically no. Some aspects of the subject are exhaustively treated elsewhere, in other French national museums. The end of the 19th century and the twentieth century are properly the province of the Musée d'Orsay and the Musée d'Art Moderne, while Eastern and Far Eastern art belong to the Musée Guimet, and African and Pacific art belong to the Musée National des Arts Africains et Oceaniens. As to the various schools, cultures and techniques represented in the Louvre's collections, the museum cannot and should not pretend to be a perfect, objective and comprehensive guide. On the contrary, the Louvre's originality and special character stems not only from its richness, but also from its unevenness, its series of great works and unique masterpieces, its

star performers and supporting cast. It would be a pointless exercise to try and pick out the 'best' museum from a list including (say) the Hermitage, Leningrad and the Metropolitan Museum, New York, not to mention the separate and complementary museums of London, Berlin and the Louvre itself. Whatever these institutions have to offer is linked to the difficulties they have to face and the conditions under which their collections have been assembled. The Louvre's particular good fortune is that it has inherited a royal gallery from France's ancien régime (like those of Vienna, Madrid or Florence), composed of emblematic, often irreplaceable works. These it can display alongside acquired collections (like those of New York, London and Berlin) which have been brought together over the last 200 years through a combination of careful purchasing and providential private donations, during a period when the history of art-and connoisseurship-underwent its broadest expansion.

A priceless amenity distinguishing the Louvre from its peers is the backdrop it provides to its collections. There was always the splendid palatial architecture, with features from the 16th through to the 19th century, and the extraordinary site in the centre of the city. But today, at a single stroke, the Grand Louvre project has vastly enlarged the perspective of the museum, on the one hand in terms of the past, and on the other in terms of the present. The excavation of the Cour Carrée brought to light the monumental moat belonging to the original château of Philippe Auguste and Charles V, which epitomized the

power of the monarchy; while the Napoleon hall and courtyard fronted by I.M. Pei's pyramid, which are the first stages in the grand project to modernize the entire museum, have given the Louvre a secure place in the history of contemporary architecture.

Michel Laclotte

**Director of the Musée du Louvre**

# The Louvre Palace and Museum

The Louvre was originally a medieval fortress, built in 1200 during Philippe Auguste's reign, on a location at which Paris's defenses were the weakest. The site was called Lupara, which became Louvre in French. This location corresponds to the present site of the southwest quarter of the Square Courtyard, where a quantity of impressive remains, unearthed between 1984 and 1985, are now on view in the basement [1]. When the structure ceased to serve as a defense post, Charles V (1364-1380) enlarged it and made it into a royal residence [2]. However, its new function soon came to an end: the vicissitudes of the Hundred Years' War, and eventually the attraction of the Loire valley diverted the sovereign's attention from their capital city for over one and a half centuries.

After their return to Paris, the early fortified castle vanished. François I had its imposing keep demolished in 1527, and, in 1546, decided to replace the rest by a Renaissance style building. This undertaking was assigned to the architect Pierre Lescot, who completed it under the last Valois kings and is assumed to have drafted the plans of the new palace [3]. Whatever the case, the work was carried on over the ensuing reigns and centuries in the same spirit of classical regularity.

Catherine de' Medici commissioned Philibert Delorme and Jean Bulland to construct two galleries about 500 meters to the west, on a location known as the *Tuileries,* designed to connect the partially transformed Louvre with the palace built at the same period. These are the *Small Gallery* and the *Great Gallery,* the latter also being known as the "Riverside Gallery", associated with Henri IV (1589-1610). In the 17th century, under Louis XIII and later Louis XIV, the other buildings surrounding the present *Square Courtyard* were erected by Lemercier and Le Vau. They are flanked on the east by **Perrault's colonnade** [4].

In the early 19th century, under Napoleon I, Percier and Fontaine began the construction of the north wing, symmetrical with the Great Gallery, while also completing the quadrilateral buildings and their decoration. Half a century later, Napoleon III had Visconti and Lefuel construct the buildings bordering the **Napoleon Courtyard** [5] on the north and south, designed to complete the enclosure of the space between the early Louvre and the Tuileries. However, the Tuileries palace was burned to the ground in 1871, and the unity of the huge palatial ensemble was destroyed on the west. The only buildings that were restored were the two corner pavilions-the *pavillon de Marsan* (along the rue de Rivoli) and the *pavillon de Flore* (along the Seine), together with their immediately adjoining prolongations.

Although the Louvre Museum did not come into being until the end of the 18th century, during the French Revolution, the idea for it had been launched forty years earlier. In a pamphlet decrying the secrecy of the royal collections, Lafont de Saint-Yenne had recommended that the latter be displayed to the public in the palace's Great Gallery. In response to this recommendation, which was echoed by other writers and

**[1] Vestiges of the medieval château**
*In the foreground: the tower on the north-east corner, known as the "Tour de la Taillerie"*

**2** The medieval Louvre: detail of the "Retable of the Paris Parliament"
*mid-15th century*

philosophers, notably by Diderot in his *Encyclopédie* (in the article entitled *"Le Louvre"*, 1765), an initial project was unsuccessfully submitted to Louis XV by the Marquis de Marigny, director of buildings. The idea was taken up again under Louis XVI and studied attentively by Count d'Angiviller, Marigny's successor. However, it came to naught because of financial difficulties and political events.

The Convention deserves the credit for making this dream come true after the fall of the monarchy. The Central Museum of the Arts was set up by decree on July 27th, 1793, and was inaugurated on August 10th of that year. However, this opening proved to be partial and temporary. The Great Gallery, where the paintings were exhibited, and the ground floor of the Small Gallery devoted to antiquities were gradually made ready throughout the Revolution and the First Empire, with major work actively proceeding after 1802, when Vivant Denon became the museum's managing director. The establishment was continuously enriched with objects brought back from the wars; and it was named the Napoleonic Museum in 1803, when it presented what was probably the most splendid collection of masterpieces of all time.

This collection was dispersed in 1815 by the restitutions imposed by the allies after Napoleon's downfall. However the Louvre collections were again rapidly increased under the Restoration and the July Monarchy, notably through the transfer to the palace of some of the sculptures from the Museum of French Monuments, closed in 1817, and through the continuous development of the departments of Greek, Roman, Egyptian and Oriental antiquities. The museum thus gradually spread out into the four wings of the Square Courtyard.

**3 Pierre Lescot's façade for the Square Courtyard in 1553**
*Engraving by Jacques 1ᵉʳ Androuet du Cerceau*
Bibliothèque Nationale

**4 The Louvre Palace: Perrault's colonnade**

Under the Second Empire, a further wing was constructed with the Denon pavilion at its centre. At the same time, three more buildings were added to link this new wing with the Great Gallery; together, the new display rooms formed a more viable circuit for visitors, better adapted to the quantity and variety of works exhibited. Subsequently, the museum has had to keep abreast with developments in museology, art history and archeology, not to mention the steady expansion both of its collections, and of the crowds who come to see them. Today, it is estimated that up to three million people pass through the Louvre every year. The buildings have undergone an almost continuous process of change right up to the present time, culminating with the opening of the Flore Pavilion in 1968, and (latterly) with a decision by the President of the Republic in September 1981 to restore to the museum a section of the palace occupied by the Ministry of Finance.

This decision has been one of enormous importance, for two reasons. First, it has made available a quantity of new exhibition space; and second, it holds out the possibility of a far more compact museum, easier to find one's way around than the present seven hundred metre labyrinth extending between the Flore Pavilion and the Colonnade. Today, the Louvre finally has the main entrance it has lacked for over three hundred years, complete with reception facilities at the basement level. These facilities were designed by the architect I.M. Pei, who is also responsible for the glass **pyramid** ₆ which crowns them.

The Louvre collections are divided into seven departments: Oriental Antiquities, Egyptian Antiquities, Greek, Etruscan and Roman Antiquities, Paintings, Sculptures, Objets d'Art and Graphic Arts.

**⁵ The Napoleon courtyard during the Second Empire**
*Photo by Ed. Baldus, 1857*
**Musée d'Orsay**

**6** I.M. Pei's Pyramid

# Oriental Antiquities

The Oriental Antiquities department, housed in the northern half of the ground floor of the buildings on the Square Courtyard, presents a virtually complete panorama of ancient Near Eastern civilizations. This department was created in 1881, and its history is closely linked with the development of archeological research in Mesopotamia, Iran, the Levant, Cyprus and Punic North Africa. It started with Paul-Emile Botta's excavations in Khorsabad in 1843-the objects from which enabled the founding of the Louvre's first - "Assyrian Museum" in 1847-to the contemporary findings of Claude Schaeffer at Ras-Shamra and of André Parrot at Mari, and includes notably the discoveries of the Renan mission to the Lebanon (1860), of the Persian delegation, whose first director, in 1897, was Jacques de Morgan, and of the French archeologists who explored the site of Telloh in Lower Mesopotamia from 1877 to 1933, and brought back the revelation of the Sumerian civilization.

The section devoted to early Mesopotamia, Sumer and Akkad, is especially rich. This period is illustrated by important monuments, such as the *Stele of the Vultures,* erected in 2450 by E-anna-tum, prince of Lagash, in memory of his conquests, and the no less famous one raised about 2270 by **Naram-Sin 8**, ruler of Akkad, to commemorate his victory over the barbarians of the Zagros mountains on the borders of Iran. This masterly composition depicts Naram-Sin as a god, striding up a wooded mountainside and trampling his fallen enemies underfoot. Various representations of this prince of Lagash bear witness to

the Sumerian renaissance at the end of the third millennium, during the reign of the administrator **Gudea 9**. One of them, in calcite, shows him holding a vase, a divine attribute, from which fish-filled, lifegiving water is flowing forth. Numerous objects-cylindrical seals, inscribed tablets, ornaments, weapons, vases, frescoes, paintings and sculptures-discovered at Mari testify to its history (circa 2500 to 700). In the room devoted to Mari and Larsa, an alabaster statuette, a masterpiece of Sumerian-inspired Mesopotamian art, dates from about 2500 BC. It was dedicated by the intendant **Ebih-il 7** to the goddess Ishtar. The worshipping figure is seated on a wickerwork stool and garbed in a sheepskin skirt. The inlaid eyes impart intense life to the face, and this effect is enhanced by the half-smile that seems to hover on its lips.

One object that is both a work of art and a historical document stands out in this department-and in the whole Louvre Museum-testifying more eloquently than anything else to the grandeur of the first Babylonian kingdom. This is the **Code of King Hammurabi 10** (1792-1750 Sargon BC), discovered in 1901 at Susa, where it had been brought as booty during the 12th century BC. This conical stele of basalt is 2.25 meters high and covered with cuneiform script, in the Akkadian language. It constitutes not so much a "code" as it does a compendium of common law, of exemplary statements dictated by the king "so that his country might learn firm discipline and proper conduct". At the top, a majestic scene shows Hammurabi standing in an attitude of prayer before Shamash, god of the sun and of justice.

**7** Ebih-il, intendant of Mari
*circa 2500 BC*

**8** Stele of Naram-Sin, king of Akkad
*circa 2270 BC*

**9** Gudea, with flowing vase
*circa 2150 BC*

The vestiges that testify to Assyrian might from the 9th to the 7th century BC possess a dramatic quality. Great reliefs-decorative elements from the palaces of Nimrud, Nineveh and, especially, Khorsabad-evoke the glorious deeds of the kings who raised these vast buildings, particularly those of **Sargon II 11** (721-705 BC), represented in his duties as the supreme administrator, issuing instructions to his minister. Huge sculptures hint at the immensity of the palace erected by this king at Khorsabad: **Winged bulls with human heads 12,** four meters high, are guardian spirits standing watch over the palace entrances, together with lion-taming giants.

Other collections illustrate the civilizations that flourished to the east of Mesopotamia, on the plateau to which the invading Iranians gave their name at the end of the 2nd millennium, and at the foot of this plateau. There are painted ceramics, animal-shaped vases, figures of votaries from ancient Susiana, from the sixth to the middle of the 4th millennium. Elamite works such as the massive bronze statue of *Queen Napirasu,* and the smaller *Smiling God,* which was formerly covered in gold plate, show the Mesopotamian influence on the kingdom of Susa during the third and second millennia; others, like the huge **Capital adorned with half-length bulls 13,** that topped one of the columns of the palace of Darius (521-485 BC) at Susa, testify to the grandeur of the Achaemenid kingdom of Persia. From the same building comes the glazed brick panel representing **Archers of the Guard 14,** the "Immortals", the elite of the magnificent army that was defeated by the Greeks at Marathon. Parthian terracotta pieces (200 BC-300 AD) are derived from Hellenic art, and luxury items from the Sassani period (224-651) include a **Royal bust 15** from the late 6th century AD which, in contrast, reflects the vigorous revival of Iranianism on the eve of the Arab conquest.

**10** Code of Hammurabi, king of Babylon
*1792-1750 BC*

**11** Sargon II of Assyria and one of his ministers
*end of 8th century BC*

**12** Assyrian winged bull
*Khorsabad, 8th century* BC

Numerous bronze objects from the civilizations in this area attest to the originality of the art of the high valleys of Luristan, on the eastern edge of the Iranian plateau, from the middle of the 3rd millennium to the 7th century BC, including weapons, standards, votive pins and hatchets, and **Plaques from horses' bits** 16, decorated with genii, animals and stylized monsters.

This collection ends with antiquities from the Levant. From Palestine, the Holy Land of the Bible, come numerous objects found in the Negev desert, some of which date back to the 4th millenium.

Several monuments from the Syro-Phoenician region go back to the Roman period, such as the Mithreum of Sidon and the fine ensemble of Palmyrian sculptures; others are contemporary with the Persian domination, like the sarcophagi from Sidon (5th to 4th centuries BC), which bear the unmistakable mark of the dual influence of Egypt and Ionia ; still others belong to high antiquity, such as the supremely precious pieces discovered at Byblos and, especially, at Ras-Shamra, the ancient Ugarit, the point at which the Syrian, Egyptian and Mycenean cultures met during the 2nd millennium 17.

The no less complex history of Cyprus, from the Neolithic Age (circa 4000 BC) until the Roman era, is abundantly illustrated by an abundant series of vases, terracotta figurines 18, jewelry and sculptures, while the Punic and Libyco-Punic monuments brought from Tunisia and Algeria evoke the distant past of the Phœnician civilization.

An Islamic Art section is attached to the Oriental Antiquities department, but at the moment only part of this collection is on display. Most of the objects come from Egypt, Syria and Persia, including

**13** Capital from the Apadana
*Susa, late 6th century BC*

**14** Archers of the Guard of Darius I

*Susa, 521-485 BC*

**15** Sassanid royal bust

*6th century AD*

ceramics, fabrics, carpets and metal objects such as the silver-and gold-inlaid copper bowl from Egypt or Syria known as the **Saint Louis baptistery** **19** (circa 1300).

**16** Plaque from a Luristan bridle-bit
*8th century* BC

**17** Gold cup, with wild buffalo hunt
*Ras-Shamra, 14th century* BC

**18** Mother and Child
*Cypriot idol, circa 2000 BC*

**19** Baptistery of Saint Louis
*Islamic art, circa 1300 AD*

# Egyptian Antiquities

Another department that is world-famous in the field of archeology but of earlier creation (1826) than the preceding one is the Department of Egyptian Antiquities. It has been steadily enriched by donations and purchases, while a number of French scholars, beginning with its founder and first curator, Jean-François Champollion, the decipherer of the hieroglyphics, have contributed their discoveries. Today, its collections make it possible to trace the civilization and art of ancient Egypt throughout the entire continuity of their development, from their origins down to the Christian era. They are exhibited on the ground floor of the southeast quarter of the Square Courtyard buildings, on the so-called Egyptian staircase and on the first floor of the south wing, in a series of rooms overlooking the courtyard. These rooms are known as the Charles X Museum because of the decorations executed in 1827-1833, which confer considerable historical interest upon them.

For many observers, the most attractive feature of this department is its exceptionally rich documentation on the life and customs of the ancient Nile Valley inhabitants. These are illustrated by innumerable texts, pictorial representations and all manner of everyday objects (weapons, tools, recipients, furniture, clothing, toilet articles, jewelry, games, toys, scribes' accessories, musical instruments, etc.) **20, 28, 32, 33**. The majority of the visitors, however, are chiefly interested in the brilliant array of masterpieces, some of which rank among the most famous in Egyptian art.

The first manifestation of this art is illustrated by the **Guebel-el-Arak knife 21** (circa 3300-3200 BC) whose ivory handle is adorned with war and hunting scenes. The Asian influence, predominant in the predynastic era, clearly emerges here. It was during the Thinite period, under the first two dynasties, that

**20** Trigonal harp
*Saïte period, 7th-6th centuries BC*

**21** Guebel-el-Arak knife
*predynastic period,*
*circa 3300-3200 BC*

**22** Serpent-king stele
*Thinite period, circa 3100 BC*

**23** Head of King Djedefre
*Old Kingdom, circa 2570 BC*

Egyptian sculpture acquired its own original style, achieving a high technical level as early as the first centuries of the 3rd millennium. One striking example is a limestone monument dating from around 3100 BC, from the royal necropolis at Abydos, the **Stele of King Wadji 22** the so-called Serpent King. Its restrained, majestic decoration represents the facade to the king's palace, joining a vertical projection of its surrounding walls. Inside them is sculptured a snake, the hieroglyphic sign for this king's name. The whole is topped by the image of a falcon, the sacred animal of the god Horus, incarnation and protector of the Egyptian dynasty.

The creations of this archaic era, the works of ancient Egypt (2700-2200 BC)-carved of stone or wood, statues or bas-reliefs-are outstanding for their grandeur. Under the 4th and 5th dynasties, this grandeur was enhanced by a vigorous realism, which gives a look of unmistakable veracity to the specimens in the Louvre. This is especially evident in the dark pink quartzite head of King **Djedefre 23**, which was probably part of a sphinx, or, despite their mutilated state, in the deeply moving wooden statues of a **Memphite official and his wife 24**. This concern with intensely expressing the personality of the individual portrayed is brought to a climax in one of the best known works of ancient Egypt, the **Squatting Scribe 25**. This painted figure was discovered in a chapel at Saqquara, and possibly represents Kaï, a provincial administrator of whom the department possesses another statue found in the same tomb. Anonymous or not, this personage, rush-pen in hand and papyrus spread over his lap, fascinates the beholder with his expressive physiognomy, his eyes glittering with intelligence, gazing attentively at whoever is dictating to him. The impression is enhanced by the eyes inlaid with opaque white quartz for the cor-

**24** Memphite official and his wife
*Old Kingdom, circa 2350-2200 BC*

**25** Squatting Scribe

*Old Kingdom, circa 2500 BC*

**26** Amenemhatankh,

"chief of the prophets"

*Middle Kingdom, circa 1850 BC*

nea, rock crystal for the iris and ebony for the pupil.

The Middle Kingdom (2060-1786 BC) under the 11th and 12th dynasties continued to aim at realism, but already a trend toward idealization had set in. This is demonstrated by two items in the Louvre collection: the starkly designed yet harmonious sandstone statue of **Amenemhatankh, "Chief of the Prophets"** **26**, and the stuccoed, painted wooden figure of the graceful, slender **Offering Bearer** **27**, delicately modelled under her transparent tunic overlaid with pearl netting.

The trend toward increasingly subtle idealization asserted itself under the New Kingdom (circa 1555-1080 BC), an incomparably glorious and prosperous period in the history of the Nile Valley. The absolute power of the pharaohs, the glittering life at court and the wealth of the ruling class gave rise to a truly "classic" art which best expressed the Egyptian people's ideal of beauty. In this aesthetic, grandeur and nobleness are tempered by grace and gentleness. It is not easy to choose among all the masterpieces in the department that testify to this evolution. Many visitors are attracted by the diorite statue of **Nephthys** **29**, inscribed with the name of Amenophis III (circa 1403-1365 BC). The goddess's figure is represented with sober elegance, in a standing position, pressing a papyriform sceptre against her body. Others focus on a painted limestone relief from the tomb of **Seti I** **30** (circa 1303-1290 BC), in the Valley of the Kings. It depicts the goddess Hathor in a splendid tunic, holding out to the sovereign her necklace charged with protective fluid. This is one of the finest examples showing the sensitivity and charm of the art of the New Kingdom.

A work situated chronologically between the two noted above emerges as

**27** Offering bearer
*Middle Kingdom, circa 2000-1800 BC*

**²⁸ Stele of Antef**

*high official under Thutmosis III, circa 1490-1439 BC*

**²⁹ The goddess Nephthys**

*New Kingdom, circa 1400 BC*

all the more surprising, i.e. the extraordinary sandstone bust of **Amenophis IV-Akhenaton** **31** (circa 1365-1349 BC), presented by Egypt to France in gratitude for the latter's role in saving the Nubian monuments. This huge head is representative of a brief revolution, expressed in art as well as in religion by a peculiar naturalism: it is carved so as to be seen from below-its summit is four meters above the ground-and it is typical of the official statuary of El-Amarna, the new (and ephemeral) capital of the kingdom. Here is an art animated by a deeply introspective realism, which is not afraid to exaggerate or even to commit excesses in order to reveal the intense spiritual life of the "seer" of Aton.

Other works of fine quality illustrate the efforts of Egyptian sculptors under the last native dynasties to revive the realism typical of Old Kingdom art. An elegant wooden statuette from the 30th dynasty (380-342 BC) is especially characteristic of this archaistic tendency, associated with a stylized elongation of the body. It represents a man standing, garbed in a long tunic, whose shaven head shows that he exercised some priestly function **34**.

The last days of Ancient Egypt-the Ptolemaic, Roman and Byzantine periods are also represented in the Louvre by a wide array of antiquities. Coptic art is so lavishly represented that an entire section has been devoted to it. Architectural fragments, reliefs of stone and wood, tapestries and garments, liturgical bronzes, ivories, glassware and ceramics reveal successively the pharaonic and above all Greco-Roman sources of this art, from its beginnings in the 4th century AD, its zenith during the Christian era (from the 5th to the 7th century) and, finally, after the Arab conquest (641), its prolongation down to the 12th century. The rearrangement of the Coptic collections has also made it

**30** **The goddess Hathor protecting Seti I**
*New Kingdom, circa 1300 BC*

**31** Amenophis IV Akhenaton

*circa 1365-1349 BC*

**32** Swimming girl and duck cosmetic spoon

*14th century BC*

possible to partially reconstruct, from elements of its internal and external architecture and decoration, a church that was built in the 6th century and used until at least the ninth century: that of the Saint Apollo monastery at Baouït, a village in Middle Egypt. An extremely beautiful painting on wood from the monastery chapel, depicting **Christ protecting the Abbot Mena 35** (the head of the convent, 7th century AD), has been placed near the posts of the triumphal arch.

**33** Sarcophagus of Chancellor Imenimet
(back, front and lid interior)
*8th century BC*

**34** Anonymous priest
*Late Period,*
*4th century* BC

**wood**

**35** Christ protecting Abbot Mena
*7th century* AD

## Greek, Etruscan and Roman Antiquities

The third archeological department traces its origins back to a Museum of Antiquities that was opened in the Louvre in 1800. To the royal collections in this initial foundation were added numerous works brought back from Italy after the French military victories, although only a small number remained after the restitutions effected by the allies in 1815. However, additional Greek, Etruscan and Roman antiquities soon began arriving to enrich the museum, and a steady stream of acquisitions, down to modern times, have made this department one of the main world centers of classical archeology. Its collections fill the Daru gallery, the Sphinx courtyard and the ground floor of the southwest quarter of the buildings around the Square Courtyard, as well as the rooms on the first floor of the south wing of this courtyard, overlooking the Seine, and the Henri II Room and the Bronze Room in the west wing. The new facilities envisaged by the Greater Louvre project confirm the Department of Greek, Etruscan and Roman Antiquities in the rooms and galleries it already occupies, while adding to it those areas beneath the Daru gallery which look northward across the Visconti courtyard, along with half of the first floor gallery contained by the Square Courtyard's south wing. Structural alterations for this purpose are now under way.

There is no chapter in the history of the art of antiquity, from the origins of Hellenism **36** to the last days of the Roman empire, that is not illustrated here either simultaneously or successively, and often with great distinction, by

marbles, bronzes, ceramics, gold and silver work, ivories, glasswork and frescoes.

This brilliant review is illustrated by such a large number of masterpieces of sculpture that selection is difficult. For the archaic period extending from the 7th century BC the beginning of the 5th century AD, two items are worthy of note, i.e. the Doric **Auxerre Goddess 37** and the Ionian **Hera of Samos 38**. A comparison clearly shows the difference between the two principal currents underlying Greek art. The first piece-whose name stems from the fact that it was part of a collection from the vicinity of Auxerre-is one of the earliest known examples of Greek sculpture (circa 630 BC). The small, firmly built body stands with its feet joined, sheathed in a stiff tunic, bound at the waist by a wide belt, the shoulders covered by a short cape. A heavy, Egyptian-style wig covers the head. The uncluttered starkness of the style shows that it initiated in Crete. The second piece is more recent (circa 560 BC), and the cylindrical form, attesting to a Mesopotamian influence, indicates a very different approach: the delicate modelling of barely-suggested forms, the mysterious life that seems to animate them, the lightness and elegance of the draperies are characteristic of Ionia, whence it comes. A pendant to this ancient figure of Korah, which exactly resembles it, was recently discovered in the same sanctuary at Samos. The two statues, which probably stood on a plinth brought to light by the excavation, carry identical dedications to the goddess Hera, by a certain Cheramyes. Among the other pieces in the Louvre

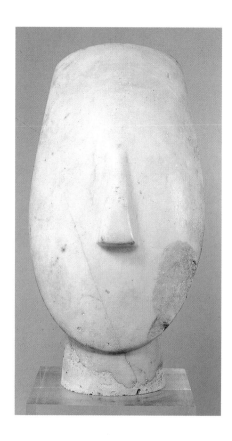

**36 Cycladic idol**
*Amorgos, second half of 3rd millennium*
marble

**37** Auxerre Goddess

*circa 620 BC*

**38** Hera of Samos

*circa 560 BC*

that bear witness to Greek archaism, mention should also be made of the **Rampin head 39** (circa 550 BC), a "masterpiece of intense delicacy and decorative charm" (J. Charbonneaux). It was part of the statue of a victorious horseman (originally in a group of two) whose torso and part of the body of whose horse are in the Acropolis Museum in Athens, along with other fragments of the ensemble.

The classical period, especially the 5th century, is represented in the Louvre collections by various pieces of high quality three-dimensional sculpture, such as the famous *Laborde Head,* which mingles gentleness, purity and energy. This head has been identified as that of the Nike driving Athena's chariot which decorated the west pediment of the Parthenon in Athens. Here again, it is through the juxtaposition of two essential works-reliefs, as it happens-that we can best understand the definitive progress accomplished by Greek art in the course of one century and the artistic characteristics of each of the two main schools from which it grew. These are a **metope 40** from the temple of Zeus at Olympia, built between 470 and 460 BC, and a fragment of the **Panathenaic procession 41** from the Parthenon, executed, like the Laborde head, between 442 and 432 BC. The strong, simple composition in intersecting diagonals of *Hercules Fighting the Cretan Bull,* the firm, robust forms of the bodies, and the somewhat stark modelling that makes the muscles seem to stand out by accentuating the shadows, are typical of the Doric technique. The *Ergastine*-sprung, like the entire decoration of the Parthenon, from Phidias's imagination-are no less characteristic of the Attic art which, in a new and harmonious way, combines the contrasting qualities of Doric and Ionic. This solemn procession of maidens who have woven the veil to be offered every four years to Athena

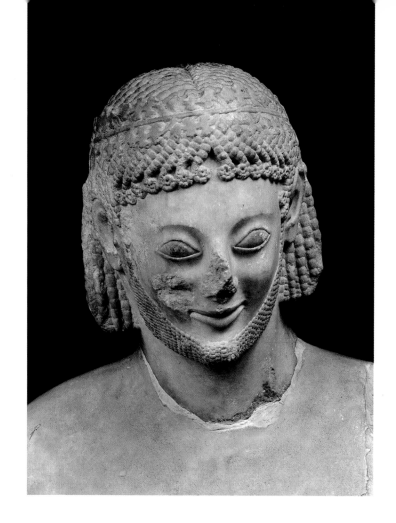

**39** Rampin head
*mid-6th century BC*

**40** Hercules and the Cretan bull

*Olympia, circa 460 BC*

**41** The Ergastines, frieze of the Panathenaics

*Parthenon, 442-432 BC*

reveals extreme care in its execution, discreet skill in its rhythm and a majesty both lively and graceful in its attitudes, which impart a feeling of true perfection.

From the 4th century on, Greek artists were increasingly attracted by truthfulness to human realities, and gradually abandoned the classical ideal. Scopas's pathos, Praxiletes's sensuality, Lysippus's heroic style paved the way for Hellenistic sculpture. Numerous works on exhibit in the Louvre testify to this evolution. Among the masculine types alone, there is the **Apollo Sauroctonus 42**, the original of which was created by Praxiteles in about 350 BC, and the **Borghese Gladiator 43**, by an artist of the first century BC, Agasias of Ephesus, clearly inspired by Lysippus.

Two statues of this period deserve mention because of their contribution to the world fame of the Louvre Museum, i.e. the **Winged Victory of Samothrace 44** and the **Venus of Milo 45**. The former, poised upright with spread wings at a galley prow, seems to be resisting the wind, which is flattening the soft folds of fabric against the body. It presumably commemorated a Rhodian naval victory at the end of the third or beginning of the 2nd century BC. At Samothrace, the 'Winged Victory' stood in a great niche towering above an "architectural landscape". Since the 1950 discovery of this statue's open right hand, it is assumed that the figure's right arm was stretched high to announce the victory. The statue of Aphrodite, an original discovered in 1820 on the island of Milo, is considered as a masterpiece of antique art and, in general, as one of the most perfect examples of female beauty. Despite the serene facial expression, which was originally thought to suggest the genius of Praxiteles, the stylistic features of this statue offer serious grounds for dating it from the late 2nd century BC. These

**42** Apollo Sauroctonus
*replica of the Praxiteles, original circa 350 BC*

**43** Borghese Gladiator
*1st century BC*

**44** The Victory of Samothrace

*late 3rd-early 2nd century BC*

features are "the proportions of the body, the fluidity of the lines, the deliberate contrast between the elaborate folds of the draperies and the nudity of the torso" (J. Charbonneaux).

A considerable amount of space in the Louvre's collections is devoted to sculptures of the Roman period. All of them demonstrate to varying degrees the artistic debt owed to Greece and the Hellenic world by Rome and its provinces. However, the numerous portraits and historical reliefs represent two branches in which there was real originality at that period. The abundant series of statues, busts and head-effigies of emperors, members of the imperial family or private citizens-constitute a veritable history of portraiture, from the time of the Republic down to the Late Empire. Some of these pieces rank among the masterpieces of the genre. They include the **Bust of Agrippa 46**, Augustu's associate and son-in-law; the basalt head of *Livia*, Augustus's wife, and the exquisitely moving head of a **Young Prince of the Antonine family 47**. Similarly, it is possible to retrace, from the late 2nd century BC to the second century AD, the evolution of the historical reliefs that constituted the main adornment of Roman commemorative buildings. The oldest, and unquestionably the most typical, of these "carved pictures" in the Louvre is the frieze that adorned one side of a large, rectangular base consecrated to the temple of Neptune in Rome, to which-presumably by mistake-was given the title of **Altar of Domitius Ahenobarbus 48** (the other three sides of this frieze are in the Munich Museum of Sculpture). It mainly depicts the sacrifice of the Suovetaurilia; on either side of the altar, in the central part, are the god Mars and a magistrate, probably in the act of consecrating it. Beside this, a fragment of the frieze of the famous **Ara Pacis 49**, the altar of peace consecrated in Rome by Augustus in 9 BC,

**45 Venus of Milo**
*late 2nd century BC*

**46** Bust of Agrippa
*early 1st century AD*

**47** Portrait of a Young Prince of the Antonine Family
*160 AD*

**48** Altar of Domitius Ahenobarbus
*(central part), end 2nd-beginning 1st century BC*

appears more Grecian because of the quality of the line, the variety of attitudes and draperies and the type of relief. The procession is nonetheless Roman, with its varied perspectives, densely clustered figures and distinctive realism; this scene is not idealized as it is in the procession of the Ergastines. The bronzes, also, are fully as important for an understanding of this sculpture-especially in the case of a masterpiece like the **Apollo of Piombino 50**, the date of which is less certain than its undisputed quality: opinions on this score vary from 500 BC to the first century AD. They help us to comprehend various aspects of the Greek, Etruscan and Roman civilizations. In the room devoted to them, statues, statuettes and small figures are displayed side by side with great numbers of other objects, interesting either because of their ornamentation, or for the purposes for which they were designed, or for both; they include **mirrors 51**, cists, lamps, armour, furniture and sundry utensils. Although Greco-Roman gold and silver work was less abundant, it is represented in the Louvre by a magnificent collection of gold jewelry and numerous silver pieces; the most famous of these were discovered at *Boscoreale,* near Pompei **52**.

Several fine examples of frescoes and, indirectly, of **mosaics 53**, testify to the quality of Greco-Roman painting, but in this realm of antique art the museum is primarily known for its vase collections. The world-famous collection of Greek vases, exhibited in the Campana Gallery-named after a very large collection purchased in 1863-provides a complete panorama of all the schools and styles, ranging from the so-called geometric ceramics (9th-8th centuries BC) to the most recent Hellenistic productions (2nd century BC) **54, 55, 56**.
These are historical documents, and also original works of art (whereas the great

**49** Frieze of the Ara Pacis
*(fragment), late 1st century BC*

**50** Apollo of Piombino

*circa 500 BC*

**51** Engraved Etruscan mirror

*3rd century BC*

majority of Greek sculptures and paintings are known only through copies dating from the Roman period). Few bear the signatures of the great masters, such as Exekias (circa 550-530 BC)-Attic red-figured vases-and Euphronios (520-500 BC)-Attic red-figured vases. The last room of this gallery houses the finest pieces of a major collection of small terracotta figures, especially known for the items crafted in the workshops of Tanagra 57 and Myrina during the Hellenistic period.

**52** Goblet from Boscoreale

*1st century AD*

**53** The Judgment of Paris, mosaic from Antioch

*2nd century* AD

**54**  Proto-Corinthian vase in the form of an owl

*7th century BC*

**55**  Bell-idol

*Boeotia, circa 700 BC*

**56** Heracles and Antaeus, wine chalice, signed by Euphronios

*circa 510 BC*

**57** The "Sophoclean Woman"

*Tanagra, end 4th century BC*

# Paintings

Although the Louvre's collection of paintings may not be the largest of any museum in the world, it is unquestionably the most complete. It originated with the "Cabinet of Pictures" constituted at Fontainebleau by François I. This collection was greatly enriched by Louis XIV-an inventory taken in 1709-1710 lists nearly fifteen hundred paintings-and, after the fall of the monarchy, it was further increased by property confiscated from the church and the émigrés, as well as by plunder from various European countries subsequent to the Revolutionary and Imperial conquests. It was considerably reduced by the restitutions made in 1815, but eventually got back into full stride, especially from the Second Empire on. Since that time there have been many donations and purchases, with the department following a policy of eclectic acquisitions in accordance with the diversity of its existing bequests. The collection occupies virtually the entire first floor of that part of the palace situated to the

Anonymous
**58** Portrait of King John the Good *circa 1360*

Jean FOUQUET
**59** Portrait of King Charles VII *circa 1445*

Enguerrand QUARTON
**60 Pietà of Villeneuve-lès-Avignon** *circa 1460*

west of the Apollo Gallery-specifically including the Square Room, the Great Gallery and the Estates Room-as well as the second floors of the west and south wings on the side of the Square Courtyard.

It is not surprising that two-thirds of the paintings in the Louvre should belong to the French school. To begin with the most outstanding items, there is, first of all, the **Pietà of Villeneuve-lès-Avignon 60**, an austere and grandiose masterpiece from the late Middle Ages, now attributed to Enguerrand Quarton, who hailed from the Laon diocese but is known to have worked in Provence from 1444 to 1446. There is also the anonymous **Portrait of King Jean the Good 58**, painted in about 1360. This is the oldest known French easel painting, as well as the first of a type for which Jean Fouquet, notably, became known during the next century, particularly through his **Charles VII 59**, in which the compact arrangement carries overtones of the Gothic style. This style of painting, in which Clouet excelled, was still flourishing in the 16th century, when the Italian decorators whom François I had brought to Fontainebleau introduced into France a mannerist art fraught with elegance and subtlety, as evidenced in **Diana the Huntress 61**, by an unknown master (circa 1550), which is thought to be an idealized portrait of King Henri II's favourite, Diane de Poitiers. Few of the painters influenced by the Fontainebleau school had such a powerful personality as Antoine Caron. His **Massacre of the Triumvirs 62**, dated 1566, is strongly allegorical, after the fashion of the day, and constitutes a barely veiled allusion to the initial horrors of the Wars of Religion.

At the outset of the 17th century, following an initial period of crisis, French artists endeavoured to revive their art directly in Italy, particularly in Rome.

Fontainebleau school
**61 Diana the Huntress** *circa 1550*

Antoine CARON
**62 Massacre of the Triumvirs** *1566*

Most of them, like Valentin and Vignon, found what they were seeking in the works of Caravaggio, with his religious themes and scenes of everyday life, and his dramatic, strongly contrasted lighting 96. Georges de La Tour was also influenced by this powerful master of European painting. He had a predilection for homely night-time interiors imbued with an atmosphere of mystery produced by the flickering light of a torch or candle, and also for a very personal simplification of forms and soberly harmonious colors, which are equally original 63, 64. The three Le Nain brothers were even more attracted by the realities of everyday life ; of the two, it was definitely Louis who, gifted with a sensitivity devoid of sentimentality, best expressed both the rusticity and the dignity of the lives of humble folk 65.

Nicolas Poussin, master par excellence of French classicism, theorist, philosopher and poet, spent nearly his entire life in Rome. More so than any other artist of his time, he was obsessed by a desire for perfection in his art, in which the landscapes that were the settings for his biblical, mythological and historical subjects eventually became his main theme 66. Claude Gellée- known as Le Lorrain-was also a "Roman" and a landscape painter, although less intellectual and more anecdotal and lyrical than Poussin. He was primarily concerned with the study of light, with its variations at different times of the day and its reflections in water 67, and he is sometimes considered as one of the precursors of Impressionism.
Portrait-painting was not neglected by French 17th-century artists, and it gave a number of rich temperaments the chance to fully express themselves.
Philippe de Champaigne, of Flemish origin, was the official painter to Louis XIII and Richelieu, and eventually became the recognized iconographer of Jansenism: his greatest masterpiece, en-

Georges de La Tour
**63** Saint Thomas *circa 1630*

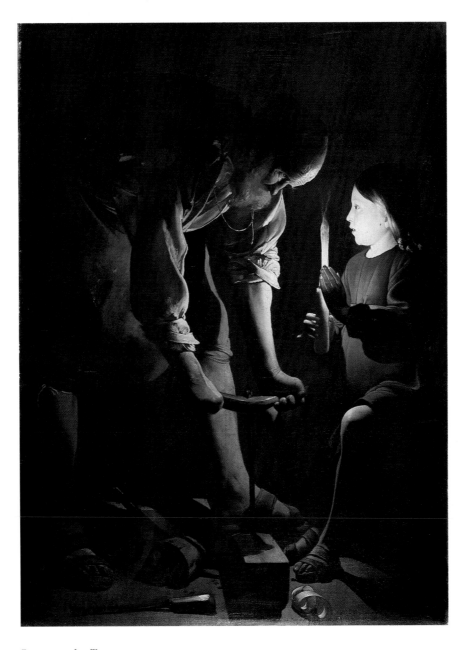

Georges DE LA TOUR
**64** Saint Joseph in the Carpenter's Shop *circa 1640*

titled **Ex-voto, 1662 68**, executed in gratitude to God for the recovery of his daughter Catherine, a nun at Port-Royal, depicts her beside Mother Agnès Arnauld at the moment at which the miracle was revealed to the abbess. This austere, fervent act of thanksgiving has little in common with the sprightly, academic manner of Charles Le Brun's *Chancellor Séguier* (circa 1655-1657) or with Hyacinthe Rigaud's solemn, sumptuous **Louis XIV 69** (1701), but both these compositions are also admirable for their subtle psychological observation of faces.

At the dawn of the 18th century, Antoine Watteau's subjects and techniques opened up new possibilities for painting. He frequently drew his inspiration from scenes and characters in contemporary French and Italian theatre plays, and his portrait of an actor, entitled **Gilles 70**, is at once symbolic and personal-it is considered by some to be a self-portrait. This delicate colorist and no less remarkable draftsman gave his genius full play by transposing these subjects into the make-believe world of dreams and pageantry. As the painter of *fêtes galantes*, he was admitted to membership in the Royal Academy of Painting and sculpture on August 28th, 1717, on which occasion he exhibited *The Pilgrimage to Cythera,* a second version of which is now in the Charlotenburg Palace in Berlin. Watteau's sensitive, poetic art set the tone for several decades of French painting. It is found in the elegant genre of François Boucher, although his art was more licentious and decorative; in that of Honoré Fragonard **71**, more intimist and executed with greater brio; and in the still-lifes and portraits **118** of Jean-Baptiste Chardin, which are linked with the trend toward realism. Even the moralistic Jean-Baptiste Greuze made a concession to the vogue for gracility when he painted **The Broken Pitcher 72** (1777).

Louis Le Nain
**65** Peasant Family *circa 1643*

Nicolas POUSSIN
**66 Shepherds in Arcadia** *circa 1640*

During the second half of the 18th century, an increasingly strong reaction set in against a style of painting that had begun to seem unduly witty, too charming, overly concerned with everyday realities. Archeological discoveries revived admiration for Greco-Roman antiquity, while at the same time there emerged a generalized idealism that demanded a simpler, more serious and more heroic type of art. This aspiration spawned the neoclassical movement, of which **The Oath of the Horatians 73**, the big success at the 1785 Salon, was a kind of manifesto. The work of Louis David contains all the elements of neoclassicism, i.e. the moral or historical grandeur of the subject, a composition with the rhythmic balance of an antique bas-relief, noble poses, anatomical precision and primary importance assigned to drawing rather than to color. The Revolution and, later, the Napoleonic epic afforded this imperious doctrinaire and his pupils a chance to give brilliant expression to their ideas. David was able to display all his talent for portrait-painting in **The Coronation 74**, done between 1805 and 1807, and **Bonaparte Visiting Victims of the Plague at Jaffa 75** was executed within the span of a few months by Antoine Gros: these are two of the Louvre's largest and most renowned canvases. In spite of this official blessing, however, neoclassicism did not reign unchallenged. The sensitivity and poetic charm of Pierre-Paul Prud'hon **76** prolonged the graceful manner of the 18th century, while foreshadowings of Romanticism were already evident in the work of Anne-Louis Girodet. Indeed, something of this same anticipation may perhaps be detected in the color and epic inspiration of the *Victims of the Plague at Jaffa*.

**The Raft of the Medusa 77**, presented at the 1819 Salon by Théodore Gericault, is often considered to be the first manifestation of French Romanticism in

Claude Gelée, *known as* LE LORRAIN
**67 Seaport** *1639*

Philippe de CHAMPAGNE
**68 Ex-voto, 1662**

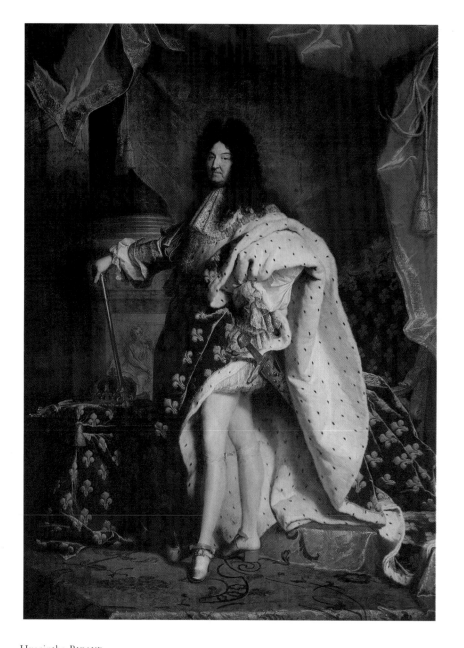

Hyacinthe RIGAUD
**69** Louis XIV in Coronation Robes *1701*

painting. This illustration of a contemporary human interest story (the survival of fifteen people shipwrecked after the sinking of a frigate that had set sail for Senegal in July 1816) is executed with a passion and dramatic force that rank it among the great masterpieces of French painting and that, in any case, justify its being displayed in the same gallery as the works of Eugène Delacroix, whose advent marked the triumph of the new school. Triumph of color, of movement, of emotion... This was a revolution, and one may justifiably wonder which of this brilliant painter's sixty-odd canvases best represent it. Many observers would cast their vote for **Freedom Guiding the People 78**, inspired by the events of July 1830, though some prefer the more sober Delacroix of *The Taking of Constantinople by the Crusaders* (1841), in which the tumultuous movement of the preceding work is moderated and harmonized by the nobility of the composition. We should also be neglecting an essential aspect of this sumptuous colorist if we failed to mention the *Women of Algiers in their Apartment* (1834), in which light plays such an important part; nor could we understand his tormented nature if we forgot the **Portrait of Frederick Chopin 79** (1838), which exposes all the anguish of romantic creation.

It is traditional to compare Delacroix with Jean-Dominique Ingres-the magician of colorful masses as against the poet of forms **119**, the admirer of the Venetians and of Rubens as against the admirer of the 15th century Florentines and of Raphael, devoted to the pure lines and subtle curves learned from the paintings on Greek vases; the ardent defender of the imagination as against the clear, realistic mind imbued with classical distinctness and honest observation. Three paintings, each in its own way, typify the aesthetic of this serene, up-

Antoine WATTEAU
**70** Gilles *circa 1718*

Honoré FRAGONARD
**71** **Women Bathing** *circa 1770*

right bourgeois who was nonetheless voluptuously inspired by the beauty of the female form. *The Apotheosis of Homer* (1827) is a composition designed to decorate a ceiling of the Louvre, where it was intended to constitute a profession of faith; the *Portrait of Monsieur Bertin* (1832), founder of the *Journal des Débats,* is an almost symbolic representation of the upper-middle class of the day; **The Turkish Bath** $_{81}$ (1862) is the synthesis and outcome of a lifetime's research devoted to the theme of women bathing. In time, an "Ingres School" also emerged; Theodore Chassériau successfully reconciled it with the art of his master's rival Delacroix, and his **Esther at her Toilet** $_{80}$ is worthy of both of them.

Romanticism revived an interest in nature, which played an important part in French painting from 1830 on. The Louvre possesses over one hundred and thirty canvases by Camille Corot, who illustrates this trend. Although he followed the classical tradition handed down by Poussin and Claude Lorrain, the poetic freshness of Corot's approach and an increasingly evident interest in the subtle play of light resulted in a freedom of plastic expression that reveals him as a forerunner of Impressionism $_{82}$. Most of the other landscape painters followed in the footsteps of the 17th-century Dutch painters; several of them settled on the edge of the Fontainebleau forest at Barbizon, which thereby gave its name to a school of painting. The most noteworthy of these, Theodore Rousseau $_{84}$, was soon followed there by Dupré, Diaz, Daubigny and Jacque. Altogether free of literary content, their landscapes exalted the beauty of nature, trees and water, with vibrant renderings of the general atmosphere, and of the variations in light at a given site at different times of the day. In so doing they anticipated the celebrated "series" of the Impressionists. Man is absent from most of the works

Jean-Baptiste GREUZE
**72 The Broken Pitcher** *1777*

Louis DAVID
**73 The Oath of the Horatians** *1784*

Louis DAVID
**74 Coronation of Napoleon I at Notre Dame de Paris, December 2nd 1804** *(détail), 1805-1807*

of the Barbizon painters, a fact that has
been seen as a denial of the modern
world, along with progress, industri-
alization and their accompanying social
difficulties. In that regard they differed
from Millet, Courbet and Daumier
whose paintings glorified the lives of
peasants and city-dwellers (these now
hang in the Musée d'Orsay).

Antoine GROS
**75 Bonaparte Visiting Victims of the Plague at Jaffa** *1804*

Pierre-Paul PRUD'HON
**76 The Empress Joséphine** *1805*

Théodore GÉRICAULT
**77 The Raft of the Medusa** *1819*

Eugène DELACROIX
**78 Liberty Guiding the People** *1830*

Eugène DELACROIX
**79 Portrait of Frederick Chopin** *1838*

Théodore Chassériau
**80 Esther at her Toilet** *1842*

Jean-Dominique Ingres
**81 The Turkish Bath** *1862*

Camille COROT
**82 Souvenir de Mortefontaine** *1864*

Camille COROT
**83 Lady in Blue** *1874*

Théodore ROUSSEAU
**84** Road Leading out of the Forest of Fontainebleau

Of all the foreign schools, the Italian is best represented in the Louvre, partly because it provided the first, sumptuous royal collections of paintings, but also because it has always been highly appreciated in France. Every phase of its evolution, from the second half of the 13th century to the end of the 18th, is illustrated here by several world-famous masterpieces.

Two large panels, both from the church of San Francesco in Pisa, bear brilliant witness to the early days of Florentine art. One is Cimabue's majestic **Madonna of the Angels 85** (circa 1270), marking the onset of a reaction against the hieratism of Byzantine models in the freer, more human poses of the figures. The other is Giotto's *Saint Francis of Assisi receiving the Stigmata* (circa 1300), in which the artist achieved complete liberation. *The Bearing of the Cross,* executed by Simone Martini during his stay at the papal court in Avignon (1340-1344), is one wing panel of a small portable polyptych, the other elements of which are in the Musée Royal des Beaux-Arts in Antwerp and the Berlin-Dahlem museum. This painting, among those of the early masters of other Italian schools, exemplifies the significant contribution made by the artists of Siena.

During the *quattrocento* (15th century), under the dual influence of architecture and sculpture, Italian painting began to evolve in the direction of the Renaissance. Although Fra Angelico's **Coronation of the Virgin 87**, painted in 1434-1435 for the church of San Domenico in Fiesole, remains medieval in its choice of subject and mystic treatment, it points to a new orientation in the Louvre's collections. The scope and balance of its structure, the observance of perspective, the arrangement of the figures without regard for traditional organization-all these are clearcut signs of a modernism that becomes even

CIMABUE
**85** Madonna of the Angels *circa 1270*

GIOTTO
**86 Saint Francis Preaching to the Birds**
*predella of the retable in the church
of Saint Francis of Assisi, circa 1300*

Fra ANGELICO
**87 The Coronation of the Virgin** *1434-1435*

more obvious in the scenes from the life of Saint Dominic shown in the predella. Paolo Uccello also emerged as an innovator when, in 1455, commissioned by the Medici family, he painted the episode from **The Battle of San Romano 88**, now in the possession of the Louvre: a second episode hangs in the Uffizi Galleries in Florence, while a third is in London's National Gallery. The care with which depth and volume are rendered by bold foreshortening, the decorative stylization of the forms, emphasized by bold coloring, give this work the monumental appearance of a high-relief. **The Calvary 89**, painted by Andrea Mantegna to decorate the central part of the predella of an altar-piece for the church of San Zeno, in Verona-its lateral parts are in the museum of Tours-is more finely wrought, more geometrical, more insightful. By Sandro Botticelli, who was torn between Christianism and humanism, there are two major compositions characterized by his sharp, sinuous brushstroke, his delicate, transparent colors, and his extremely refined style, ideally suited for expressing the mannered grace of mournful, mysterious allegories. These frescoes **90**, datable 1483, come frome the Villa Lemmi (near Florence), originally the property of the Tornabuoni family, friends of the Medicis.

The so-called Golden Age (late 15th to mid-16th century) of the Italian Renaissance is brilliantly illustrated in the Louvre. First and foremost, it boasts an array, unparalleled elsewhere in the world, of works by Leonardo da Vinci, beginning with the most universally admired and discussed of all paintings, the **Mona Lisa 91**. This portrait, which may reasonably be assumed to represent Mona Lisa Gherardini, who in 1495 was married to the Florentine patrician Francesco del Giocondo, is also known as *La Gioconda*. Leonardo da Vinci was so attached to this painting, done bet-

Paolo UCCELLO
**88** The Battle of San Romano *circa 1450-1455*

Andrea MANTEGNA
**89** Calvary *1459*

Sandro BOTTICELLI
**90** Fresco from Villa Lemmi *(détail), circa 1483*

ween 1503 and 1506, that he brought it with him when François I invited him to France in 1516. He settled near Amboise, in the Château de Cloux, where he died three years later. The *Mona Lisa* thereupon became the most precious item in the king's "Cabinet of Paintings". Virtually everything has been said about the enigmatic smile, the marvelous modelling of the face, the shading off of the color values so that the light seems to glide over the forms, the misty, dreamlike atmosphere of the background landscape. In the same way, the mysterious poetry and the already perfect craftsmanship of the *Virgin of the Rocks,* commissioned in 1483 by the Brotherhood of the Conception of San Francesco Grande in Milan, have been the subject of continuous study. The same is true of the symbolism and spirituality of **The Virgin, the Child and Saint Anne 92**, a painting executed several years after the *Mona Lisa* and commissioned by the Servites of Florence for the high altar of their church.

Several of the paintings by Raphael that now hang in the Louvre once belonged to François I. This was presumably the case for **The Virgin and Child with Saint John the Baptist 93**, which, because of the rusticity of the scene, is traditionally known as *La Belle Jardinière.* All in all, it is the finest example in the museum's collections of the perfect harmony to which its artist aspired. A freer-style portrait painted by Raphael in 1514-1515 is hardly less well-known: it represents his friend *Balthazar Castiglione,* a poet and diplomat and "the finest knight in all the world", according to Emperor Charles V. Louis XIV acquired it from Mazarin's heirs in 1661. In the same year and from the same source, Correggio's *Antiope* (circa 1524-1525) was purchased for the royal collections. This work was well known in its day and its artistry is less intellectual, more relaxed in its sensuality.

Leonardo DA VINCI
**91** **The Mona Lisa** *circa 1503-1506*

Leonardo DA VINCI
**92** The Virgin, the Child and Saint Anne *circa 1506-1510*

This latter tendency eventually prevailed in Venice, where, until the end of the 16th century, the Venetian artists painted not for reasons of piety or to test their abilities, but simply to give direct expression to what they felt when viewing a landscape, draperies, or naked human flesh. In the place of the fineness of line and delicate modelling beloved of the Florentines, they preferred masses of light and color. This *maniera moderna* had Giorgione as its initiator and his pupil Titian as its most illustrious representative. Is the *Rustic Concert* the work of the master or of his disciple? It is dated 1510-1511 and was long attributed to Giorgione, but nowadays is viewed as being in all likelihood by Titian. Whatever the case, stylistic comparison reveals its close resemblance to the latter's **Entombment 94**, painted some fifteen years later and added to the royal collections, together with the *Rustic Concert,* in 1671. The Louvre possesses two outstanding examples of the decorative style splendidly developed by the Venetian painters of the following generations: Veronese's gigantic **Marriage at Cana 95**, which was commissioned in 1562 and completed in 1563 for the refectory of the San Giorgio Maggiore convent in Venice, and the sketch for the huge composition entitled *Paradise,* commissioned from Tintoretto in 1588 to adorn the Great Council Hall of the Serenissime in the palace of the Doges.

Toward the end of the 16th century a new kind of art began to develop in Italy. In 1585, in Bologna, the Carracci brothers founded an academy-the first school of fine arts-where they taught a more eclectic approach. This tended toward naturalism in Annibale Carracci's landscapes entitled *The Hunt* and *The Fishing Expedition,* in the Louvre. Caravaggio was more revolutionary, and his aesthetic and technique were to exert a strong influence over European painting, especially in France. His **Death of**

RAPHAEL
**93** The Virgin and Child with Saint John the Baptist *also known as* **La Belle Jardinière**
*1507*

TITIAN
**94 The Entombment** *circa 1525*

the Virgin [96], commissioned in 1605 for
Rome's church of Santa Maria in
Trastevere, created a scandal because of
what was regarded as overly plebeian
realism accentuated by an unduly dramatic contrast between the zones of
light and shadow. All this notwith-
standing, this painting compelled admiration from those who recognized it as
foreshadowing a regeneration.

Eighteenth-century Venice witnessed the
last great days of Italian painting. Of
the works from this period in the
Louvre, the most noteworthy are those
of Francesco Guardi [97], represented by
a series of ten canvases-out of the original twelve-commemorating the festiv-
ities attendant upon the coronation of a
doge, Alvise Mocenigo IV.

VERONESE
**95** **The Marriage at Cana** *(détail), 1563*

CARAVAGGIO
**96** **The Death of the Virgin**
*circa 1605*

Francesco GUARDI
**97** **The Doge at Santa Maria della Salute** *circa 1770*

Although the Flemish and Dutch schools are less abundantly represented than the Italians in the Louvre, the museum does boast a large number of masterpieces from these two schools, of sufficient importance to provide an almost complete panorama.

From the earliest Flemish painters, the Louvre has two paintings of capital importance: Jan van Eyck's **Virgin of Autun** **98** (circa 1435), which comes from the collegiate church of that city (to which it had been donated by Nicolas Rolin, chancellor of Burgundy); and Rogier van der Weyden's *Braque Triptych* (circa 1452), probably executed for Catherine of Brabant in memory of her late husband, Jehan Braque. Among the works of the latter half of the 15th century, several paintings by Hans Memling deserve mention, notably his **Portrait of an Old Woman** **99** (circa 1470-1475). The 16th century works include **The Moneylender and his Wife** **100** (1514), by Quentin Metsys-one of the pioneer examples of genre painting in the Netherlands-and Pieter Breughel the Elder's **Beggars** **101** (1568), which has been interpreted as an allusion to the so-called "beggars' revolt" against the government of Philip II of Spain. Peter-Paul Rubens's supremacy in the Flemish school of the 17th century is brilliantly illustrated by the two admirable portraits of his second wife, Helena Fourment, and his children; by *The Village Fair* (circa 1635-1638), replete with teeming life, which was studied to advantage by several French artists (Watteau, Fragonard, Delacroix...); and, most importantly, by the huge decorative ensemble executed between 1622 and 1625 in honor of Queen Marie de' Medici, designed at her request to adorn a gallery in the Luxembourg palace. One of its best-known sections-another source of inspiration for the French artists noted above-is that entitled **Marie de' Medici Landing at Marseilles** **102**. Of the

Jan van EYCK
**98** **The Virgin of Autun** *circa 1435*

Hans MEMLING

**99 Portrait of an Old Woman** *circa 1470-1475*

Quentin METSYS

**100 The Moneylender and his Wife** *1514*

many portraits of Charles I of England by Anton van Dyck, "painter in ordinary to the king", the one in the Louvre **103** is considered to be the finest. Similarly, the painting entitled *The Four Evangelists* is regarded as one of the most outstanding canvases from Jacob Jordaens's early period.

Pieter BREUGHEL the Elder
**101** **The Beggars** *1568*

Peter Paul RUBENS
**102** **Marie de Medici landing at Marseilles** *1622-1625*

Anton VAN DYCK
**103 Portrait of Charles I of England** *circa 1635*

In the Dutch collection, all the great names are excellently represented. They include Hieronymus Bosch, with his panel painting entitled **The Ship of Fools** 104, dating from the late 15th century, a semi-surrealist allegory stigmatizing the "follies" of taste and hearing and, more generally, the vices of the painter's time. Lucas van Leyden's fantastic landscape entitled *Lot and his Daughters* (circa 1509-1517) is a mannerist-style forerunner of the following century's Dutch "luminism". By Frans Hals there is a so-called "character portrait", **The Gypsy Girl** 105 (circa 1628), reminiscent of Caravaggio in its freedom and audacity. The subtle perfection of light, color and brushwork in Jan Vermeer of Delft is represented by **The Astronomer** 107 (1688- acquired by dation in 1983), and by the subtle perfection of light, color and brushwork in his **Lacemaker** 106 (1664) which admirably expresses the serenity of domestic life by bringing out its innate poetry. Elsewhere, Jacob van Ruisdael's *The Burst of Sunlight* is rightly classed among the world's greatest landscape paintings. The pride of this collection is the impressive array of Rembrandts: portraits, especially **self-portraits** 109, like the supremely moving one in which the artist depicts himself aged fifty-four, worn out by grief, hardship and solitude, yet still confident of his art; biblical scenes, including the famous *Pilgrims at Emmaus* (1648), in which the magical chiaroscuro and the utter simplicity of the composition combine to render the divine presence visible with an intensity seldom achieved by any artist; and **Bathsheba at her Toilet** 108 (1654), showing the subject holding the letter in which David declares his love. This is one of Rembrandt's rare nudes, for which his model was his devoted second wife, Hendrickje Stoffels.

Hieronymus BOSCH
**104** **The Ship of Fools** *circa 1490-1500*

Frans HALS
**105** **The Gypsy Girl** *1628-1630*

Jan VERMEER of Delft
**106** The Lacemaker *1664*

Jan VERMEER of Delft
**107** The Astronomer *1668*

REMBRANDT
**109** Portrait of the Painter in his Old Age *1660*

The collection of German paintings is more modest, but it does feature several major items from the most glorious period of this school (late 15th century), including notably *The Descent from the Cross,* which formed the central part of a great triptych executed circa 1500 by the artist known as the Master of Saint Bartholomew (from the name of a retable in the Munich Museum); Albert Dürer's **Self-Portrait 110** painted when the artist was aged twenty-two (1493), reportedly for his fiancée (he is holding a species of thistle, symbol of fidelity); a charming *Venus* (1529) by Lucas Cranach the Elder; Hans Holbein the Younger's most famous portrait, that of **Erasmus 111**, the "prince of humanism" (1523), writing his *Commentary on the Gospel of Saint Mark.*

Similarly, even though it has only a small place in the Louvre, the English school is brilliantly illustrated. For the 17th century, there are portraits by Sir Joshua Reynolds **102**, founder of the Royal Academy; by his rival, Thomas Gainsborough; and by Sir Thomas Lawrence, painter to all the European courts. For the 19th century, there are the romantic landscapes of John Constable, Richard Parkes Bonington and Joseph M.W. Turner.

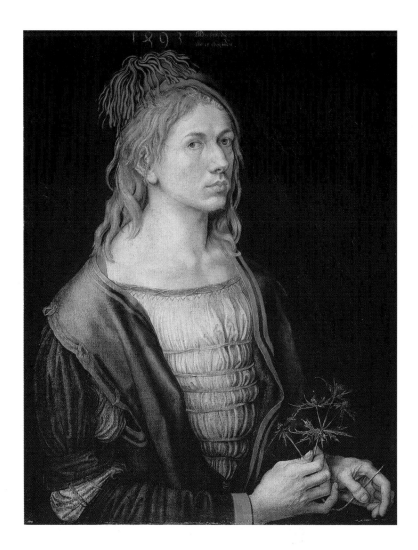

Albrecht DÜRER
**110** Self-Portrait *1493*

Hans HOLBEIN the Younger
**111** **Portrait of Erasmus** *1523*

Sir Joshua REYNOLDS
**112** **Master Hare** *1788-1789*

The Spanish collection is unquestionably less magnificent than the one that was Louis-Philippe's personal property; which, after being exhibited in the Louvre from 1838 to 1848, followed the king to his exile in London, where it was dispersed at auction in 1853. Today, it is still notable for a fine array of masterpieces: early-master paintings, such as Martorell's *Martyrdom of Saint-George* (circa 1430-1435); El Greco's **Christ on the Cross** ₁₁₃ (circa 1580), highly typical of this artist's manner; and fine examples of Spain's artistic Golden Age (17th century), such as Ribera's *Clubfooted Boy* (1642); Zurburán's **Funeral of St. Bonaventura** ₁₁₄ (about 1630; Murillo's *Beggar Boy* (1650); The portrait (attributed to Velázquez) of The Infanta Margarita, Philip IV's daughter (circa 1655); and Carreño de Miranda's *Mass for the founding of the Order of the Trinitarians* (1666). Last but not least, there are several portraits by Goya, including the splendid **Marquesa de la Solana** ₁₁₅ (circa 1791-1794).

El Greco
**113 Christ on the Cross** *circa 1580*

Zurbaràn
**114 The Funeral of Saint Bonaventure** *1629*

GOYA
**115** Portrait of the Marquesa de la Solana *circa 1791-1794*

# Graphic Arts

The Louvre's store of drawings, along with its ensemble of engravings from the Edmond de Rothschild Collection, is located in the Flove wing of the museum. This collection is so rich and varied that only a few of its treasures can be displayed at a time. Those not on display are carefully stored for protection against variations of light and temperature, but may be viewed by amateurs who have obtained the authorization of the curator's office. Temporary exhibitions on specific themes are regularly organized in a room adjoining the main collection; these may be visited by the general public during ordinary museum opening hours.

Leonardo DA VINCI

**116** **Isabelle d'Este** *circa 1490*

black chalk, red chalk and pastel

REMBRANDT

**117** **The Canal at Amersfoort** *circa 1655*

pen-and-ink and brown wash drawing

Jean-Baptiste CHARDIN
**118  Self-portrait with green eyeshade** *1775*
pastel

Jean Dominique INGRES
**119  The Stamaty Family** *1818*
black lead pencil drawing

# Sculptures

The sculpture department came into being when the Museum of French Monuments was discontinued in 1817, under the Restoration. Part of its collection was thereupon moved from the convent of the Minor Augustinians to the Louvre, and it has been continuously added to so that it now constitutes as complete a history as possible of French sculpture, from its origins to the end of the 19th century. The exhibits are arranged in chronological order on the ground floor of the building parallel to the Seine, from the entrance to the Carrousel to the Flore wing, as well as on the ground floor of the latter.

First, there are the Romanesque sculptures, most of them executed strictly on the basis of the architectural fragments they adorn. One example is the representation of **Daniel in the Lions' Den** **120**, from the late 11th century, on a recarved capital from the church of Sainte Geneviève, in Paris. This scene was obviously drawn from an Eastern model, taken from a design on some Sassanid fabric. Another is *The Prophet,* placed against a column from the cloister of Notre-Dame-des-Doms, in Avignon, from the latter half of the 12th century, in which can be detected the influence of the Royal Portal of Chartres cathedral. The style of these works is crude, but their purity and artlessness enhance the intensity of the expressions, as will be seen in the grieving **Head of Christ** **121**, in painted and gilded wood, from the first half of the 12th century, originating in Lavaudieu in the Haute-Loire, or in the grave, rustic **Virgin of Auvergne** **122**, instrument of the In-carnation and the Word, from the latter half of the century.

The column-statues from the old Notre-Dame church in Corbeil-*Solomon* and, particularly, the **Queen of Sheba** **123** (circa 1180-1190)-emerge as the last glimmerings of great Romanesque art, and herald the advent of the more brilliant, flexible and appealing Gothic style. This is represented in the Louvre by an array of masterpieces sufficiently complete to enable the beholder to follow its evolution from beginning to end : pieces from the major 13th-century stone-carving centers, such as the figure of Sainte Geneviève that adorned the pier of the old Paris church of which she was the patron saint; the fragment of the jubé from Chartres cathedral depicting *Saint Matthew the Evangelist* writing at an angel's dictation; 14th century figures of the Virgin and Child, such as the *Ryaux Virgin* from Lorraine and the Norman **Maisoncelles Virgin** **124**; and recumbent and standing effigies of sovereigns. Among the latter is a jovial figure of **Charles V** **125**, which was probably intended to adorn the East Gate of the old Château du Louvre; this is one of the most remarkable pieces of medieval portrait sculpture in existence. The patronage of Duke Jean de Berry is evidenced by the Apostle's Head, attributed to Jean de Cambrai, from the church of Mehun-sur-Yèvre (Cher). The display ends with a presentation of 15th century French and Burgundian sculptures, grouped around one of the Louvre's most celebrated masterpieces, the **Tomb of Philippe Pot** **126**; Philippe Pot was the Grand Seneschal of Burgundy. This

**120** Daniel in the Lions' Den
*Paris, late 9th century*

**121** The Christ of Lavaudieu
*second quarter 12th century*

**122** Virgin of Auvergne
*second half 12th century*

**123** The Queen of Sheba
*Corbeil, circa 1180-1190*

piece, representing a funeral cortège, was sculpted sometime between 1477 and 1483 by an "ymagier", probably Antoine le Moiturier, for the abbey church of Citeaux.

During the 16th century, French sculpture underwent the influence of the Italian Renaissance, and became more delicate, subtler, less naive. Concurrently, it also became more ornamental, and blossomed forth with decorative elements from the trans-alpine repertory. Perhaps the monument that best represents its complex evolution over the first few decades is the **Saint George 127** retable, executed in Tours for the upper chapel of the château de Gaillon by Michel Colombe, one of the last Gothic *imagiers:* this featured a new-style framework sculpted for it on the site by stone carvers from an Italian workshop. The triumph of the classical Renaissance during the second half of the century is illustrated by a series of outstanding pieces, such as Jean Goujon's bas-reliefs for the **Fountain of the Holy Innocents 128** (1547-1549), adorned with nymphs and tritons whose sensuality is unquestionably pagan; Pierre Bontemps's funeral statue of *Admiral Philippe Chabot* (circa 1570), depicting him in a recumbent position borrowed from Etruscan statuary; Germain Pilon's **Three Graces 129**, designed for the monument that contained Henri II's heart (between 1560 and 1566), inspired by a famous antique group; and this same artist's statue of *Cardinal de Birague* kneeling in prayer (1584-1585), in which the decorative fullness of the great robe's folds foreshadows the more kinetic art of the following century.

French 17th-and 18th-century sculpture was marked by sundry successive and contrasting trends-classic, realist, mannerist, baroque-and is amply represented in the Louvre. It yielded triumphal monuments, such as the one that, in

**124** The "Maisoncelles" **Virgin and Child**
*first third 14th century*

**125** Charles v (*détail*)
*Paris, circa 1390*

Antoine le MOITURIER
**126 Tomb of Philippe Pot** *last quarter 15th century*

1643, was erected near the Pont-aux-Changes, designed to accommodate the bronze effigies of Louis XIII, the young Louis XIV and **Queen Anne of Austria 130**, sculpted by Simon Guillain; funeral monuments, such as the elegant obelisk designed circa 1663 by François Anguier for the Celestine chapel in Paris to commemorate the *Dukes of Longueville;* statues designed to adorn parks, like Puget's **Milon of Crotona 131** (1682), for Versailles, and the four equestrian groups executed by Coysevox (1706) and Guillaume Coustou (1745) **132**, for Marly; pieces designed to mark a sculptor's admission into the French Academy, such as Pigalle's graceful figure of **Mercury Attaching his Heel-wing 133** (1744) and Falconnet's no less famous *Woman Bathing* (1755); and, last but not least, portraits, the long series of which ends with Houdon's rich, varied work **134**.

The neoclassicism of the Revolutionary and Imperial periods initiated by the Venetian Canova **135** was followed by a variety of trends rooted in a renewed familiarity with Antiquity and fresh interest in the Middle Ages. Passion became something to be expressed. Giraud's *Monument to his dead wife and child* is an eloquent example of this development. Sculptors did not turn to Romanticism till later. The most vigorous representatives of this trend were Barye, an exact observer of the animal world **136**; Pradier **137**; and Rude, whose **Neapolitan Fisherman 138** directly foreshadows the work of Carpeaux, now at the Musée d'Orsay.

For the purpose of pinpointing the pattern of development of sculpture, at least for the 15th and 16th centuries, and also for purposes of comparison, there is an accompanying display of works by sculptors from the contemporary schools in neighboring countries, including the Netherlands, Germany, Spain and especially Italy. Among these

Michel COLOMBE
**127** St. George Slaying the Dragon *early 16th century*

Jean GOUJON
**128** Bas-relief from the Fountain of the Holy Innocents *1547-1549*

German PILON
**129** Three Graces *circa 1560*

Simon GUILLAIN
**130** Anne of Austria *1643*

are two world-famous masterpieces by Michelangelo, the **Dying Slave** 139 and the *Rebel Slave,* sculpted from 1513 to 1515 for the tomb of Pope Julius II. They were eventually withdrawn from the monument in its final form and presented by the artist to his friend Roberto Strozzi, who offered them in homage to King Henri II of France; he in turn gave them to the High Constable de Montmorency. They remained in the latter's residence at Ecouen until 1632, when they became the property of Cardinal de Richelieu, who housed them in his château in Poitou, whence his nephew, Marshal de Richelieu, had them moved to his Paris mansion in 1749. In 1792, the statues passed into the custody of the Museum of French Monuments and from there to the Louvre, in 1794. These figures were generally assumed to be allegories of the liberal arts reduced to powerlessness by the demise of the pope, their protector. However, the prevailing opinion today is that, like the images of captives on antique triumphal arches, they were probably designed to symbolize, on the monument's lower part, the "terrestrial counterpart of the sovereign pontiff's apotheosis, depicted in the upper part". Be that as it may, and despite their unfinished state-or perhaps even because of it-the compelling, tortured loveliness of these statues imparts intense expression, in a new manner, to Michelangelo's personal anguish at the time when he was at a height of his genius.

Pierre PUGET
**131** Milon of Crotona *1682*

Jean-Baptiste PIGALLE
**133** Mercury *1744*

Guillaume COUSTOU
**132** **Horses of Marly** *1739-1745*

Jean-Antoine HOUDON
**134** **Louise Brongniart at five years old**
*1777*

Antonio CANOVA
**135** Psyche and Cupid *1793*

Antoine Louis BARYE
**136** **Lion Crushing a Snake** *1832-1835*

James PRADIER
**137** Satyr and Bacchante *1834*

François RUDE
**138** The Neapolitan Fisherman *1833*

Michelangelo
**139** The Dying Slave *1513-1515*

# Decorative Arts

The precious objects and items of furniture, kept in a section separate from the sculpture department since 1893, are exceptionally valuable from both the historical and artistic viewpoint. They come from the royal collections, from treasures confiscated during the Revolution, from the 1901 transfer to the Louvre of the former National Furniture Museum and from numerous bequests, donations and purchases down to the present time. Some of them are on display in the space above the Small Gallery, in the Apollo Gallery, so-called because the painter Lebrun, who in 1661 was commissioned by Louis XIV to decorate it, took as his theme the sun god, emblem of the sovereign. This theme was likewise adopted by Delacroix in 1848, when the gallery was restored by Duban, and he painted the central part of it with his *Apollo Vanquishing the Serpent Python.* The remainder are housed along the first floor of the buildings on the Square Courtyard, i.e. the east wing (colonnade rooms) and the north and west wings.

Clearly, the items displayed in the Apollo Gallery constitute, for the visitor, a feature attraction both because of the precious materials involved and because of the way in which they illustrate the glories of the history of France. Some of them were part of the French crown jewels, like the famed 137-carat "Regent" diamond, acquired in 1717 by Philippe d'Orléans, who was the regent during Louis XV's infancy and which adorned the **Crown** **153** worn by Louis at his coronation; others belonged to the coronation instruments, or "regalia", such as the golden **Sceptre** **146** sur-

mounted by a *statue of Charlemagne,* carved for Charles V in the 14th century; and still others came from the treasure of the royal abbey of Saint Denis or from that of the Order of the Holy Ghost, founded in 1578 by Henri III. However, in this array, certain pieces are first and foremost sheer works of art, including the porphyry vase, known as the **Eagle of Suger** **142** in the shape of a hierarchical eagle (silver-gilt) commissioned by Abbot Suger of Saint Denis,

**140 Harbaville Triptych**
*Byzantium, mid-10th century*
**ivory**

**141 The Charlemagne Statuette**
*9th century*
**bronze**

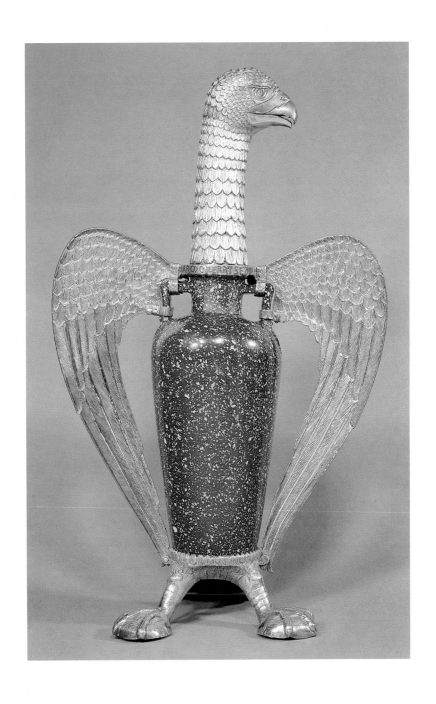

**142** Eagle of Suger
*mid-12th century*

in the 12th century; the silver-gilt **Virgin of Jeanne d'Evreux 145** presented to the abbey by the queen whose name it bears in 1339.

Of equal importance for the history of medieval and Renaissance art are the various lavish arrays of objects displayed in the Colonnade Rooms-which, in addition, house partial reconstitutions, made with their original wood panellings, of the Council Room that was in the Vincennes "château neuf" and of the King's Bedchamber and the King's State Chamber in the Louvre palace (in the Room of the Seven Fireplaces). The displays feature paleo-Christian and Byzantine ivories, such as the Berberini Ivory of an Emperor (possibly Justinian) in triumph; also the famed mid-10th century **Harbaville Triptych 140**, which contains depictions of Christ, the Virgin, Saint John the Baptist, the apostles and saints, all portrayed in the precise, sophisticated style of the day; Romanesque and Gothic ivories, including two outstanding works produced in Paris during the third quarter of the 13th century, the **Descent from the Cross** and the enchanting Virgin, a model of refinement and elegance, from the treasury of the Sainte-Chapelle; handsome specimens of medieval gold- and silver craftwork, such as the silver-gilt *reliquary triptych* from the Floreffe abbey, in Belgium (after 1254) and the reliquary arms of Saint Louis of Toulouse and Saint Luke made of crystal and enamelled silver gilt, reputedly crafted in Naples in 1337 ; Romanesque and Gothic chased-enamel pieces, such as the **Resurrection armilla (armband) 144** from a Meuse-region workshop (circa 1175-1180); the plate depicting *The Death of the Virgin,* and the *Alpais Ciborium,* from a Limousin atelier (circa 1200-1210); 16th-century painted enamels, including certain items produced by the great Limoges enameller Leonard Limosin, in particular his portrait of the

**143** **Descent from the Cross**
*Paris, 2nd half of the 13th century*
ivory

**144** **Ceremonial armband (armilla) : The Resurrection**
*Meuse, circa 1175-1180*
gilt and enamel on copper

**145** Virgin of Jeanne d'Evreux

*Paris, pre-1339*

**silver-gilt**

**146** Sceptre of Charles V

*before 1380*

High Constable **Anne de Montmorency 149**, framed with the emblems of the latter's office; Hispano-Moorish, Italian and French ceramic pieces from the 14th, 15th and 16th centuries ; medieval bronzes-the oldest of which is the renowned equestrian figure known as the **Charlemagne statuette 141** (9th century), from the Metz cathedral treasure-including a large number of Italian Renaissance bronzes, notably some by the Master of Padua, **Andrea Riccio 147**; and, lastly, a number of tapestries, including the Last Judgement, woven in Brussels circa 1500-1515, and, from that same city, circa 1530, the outstandingly splendid series devoted to **Maximilian's Hunting Expeditions 148**, woven from designs by Bernard van Orley.

The first floor of the north wing of the Square Courtyard, along with part of the west wing, is devoted to displays of French decorative art from the 16th century to 1850. The collection includes late 16th century and 17th century French and Italian bronzes, such as the statues of **Henri IV** and **Marie de Medici 151** by Barthélémy Prieur, as well as works by John of Bologna and his disciples. These objects are displayed against a remarkable backdrop of early 17th century tapestries made in Paris from cartoons by Vouet. The hangings in the "Effiat Room" nearby illustrate scenes from the *History of Scipio;* they were made at the Gobelins factory, which was founded in 1662. Also in this room are pieces of furniture from the mid-17th century: an ebony cabinet, bed and armchair. The next two rooms are devoted to the art of André-Charles Boulle, the great cabinetmaker of Louis XIV who worked at the Louvre and specialized in copper and tortoiseshell marquetry with gilded bronze appliques. The David-Weill and Niarchos galleries nearby contain masterpieces of the French goldsmith's craft in the 16th century, such as **Charles IX's** enamelled

Andrea RICCIO
**147 Arion** *(Padua, circa 1500)*
bronze

**148** The Month of August *(detail),* tapestry from the "Hunts of Maximilian" series
*Brussels, circa 1530*

Léonard LIMOSIN
**149 The High Constable Anne de Montmorency**
*1566*

enamel on copper

**150 Helmet and shield of Charles IX**
*Paris, circa 1572*

gold helmet and shield **150**; 17th century pieces such as the Gold Chest, thought to have belonged to Anne of Austria; rocaille works, notably the **Table-center of the Duc de Bourbon 154**; and various items from the neo-classical period. After this, a succession of rooms offer Louis XV furniture, especially the work of Charles Cressent, cabinetmaker to the Regent and creator of the celebrated **Monkey Commode 155**, and a fine series of broad desks inlaid with rare woods and lacquers and covered in rocaille bronzework. Towards 1760, the lines of furniture beacame more rigid in aspect, in response to the vogue for neo-classicism, while bronzework increasingly took its cue from the Greco-Roman example. This trend is chiefly represented by the work of Jean-François Deben (who made convertible furniture like the *Burgundy table* shown here), and by his disciples Jean-François Leleu and Jean-Henri Riesner. Leleu's commode for the Prince de Condé's bedroom in the Palais Bourbon is displayed against a background of Gobelins tapestries from the same building, while Riesner was responsible for much of the collection of Marie-Antoinette's furniture held by the Louvre. Louis XVI boiseries are represented by an extensive ensemble from the Hotel de Luynes on the Rue Saint-Dominique, Paris; and the "Chinese room" contains furniture lacquered in the oriental style by Martin Carlin **156**, for the daughters of Louis XV. Lastly, the rooms in the half-wing on the west side, which were occupied by the Council of State following the Restoration, all have painted ceilings dating from that time. These rooms contain displays of furniture and objects d'art from the First Empire (**Napoleon's "Athenienne" 157**, the *Empress Joséphine's jewel cabinet*, 1809); the Restoration (*Bed of Charles X*, 1825); and the July Monarchy (**Grape-Harvest Bowl 158** by Froment-Meurice).

Barthélémy Prieur
**151** Henri IV and Marie de Medicis
*Paris, circa 1610*

**152** Bed of Marshal d'Effiat
*mid-17th century*

**153** Louis XV's coronation crown
*Paris, 1722*

Jacques RöETTIERS
**154** Table-center of the Duc de Bourbon
*Paris, 1736*

silver

Charles CRESSENT
**155** **Monkey Commode**
*Paris, circa 1735-1740*

Martin CARLIN
**156** **Commode**
*Paris, circa 1780*

Japanese lacquer and gilded bronze

Martin-Guillaume BIENNAIS
**157** Napoleon 1's "Athenienne" from the Tuileries
*Paris, early 19th century*

François-Désiré FROMENT-MEURICE
**158** Grape-Harvest Goblet
*Paris, circa 1844*
agate and enamelled silver

All photography provided by : Réunion des musées nationaux
(D. Arnaudet, M. Bellot, G. Blot, M. Coursaget, C. Jean, C. Rose,
J. Schormans)
ill. 6 : © EPGL - Architecte I.M. Pei - RMN

This book was printed by the Imprimerie Hérissey,
Evreux (France) in july 1990

Premier dépôt légal : august 1989
Dépôt légal : july 1990
ISBN : 2-7118-2232-X
GG 20 2232